P9-EML-206

# *The Nature of Science*

*Bob Ritter*
*Jim Wiese*

**ITP Nelson Canada**

I(T)P An International Thomson Publishing Company

Toronto • Albany • Bonn • Boston • Cincinnati • Detroit • London • Madrid • Melbourne • Mexico City
New York • Pacific Grove • Paris • San Francisco • Singapore • Tokyo • Washington

# Contents

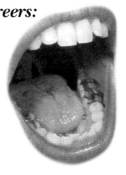

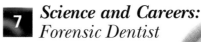

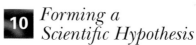

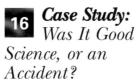

Wash hands with soap and water

Important safety information

A chance to use problem-solving skills

Design or build

A challenge

Work together

Record observations or data

Wear safety goggles

Wear an apron

# The Image of the Scientist

IF YOU WALKED INTO A CROWDED ROOM, could you pick out the scientist?

In books, movies, and on television, you will often find scientists who aren't a lot like other people. They look different. Their long words make them sound convincing, even though we cannot understand what they are saying. They always seem to have the answers. A person like this—with a mind like an encyclopedia— is intimidating. Who wouldn't be afraid to speak to a person who knows almost everything?

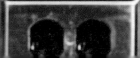

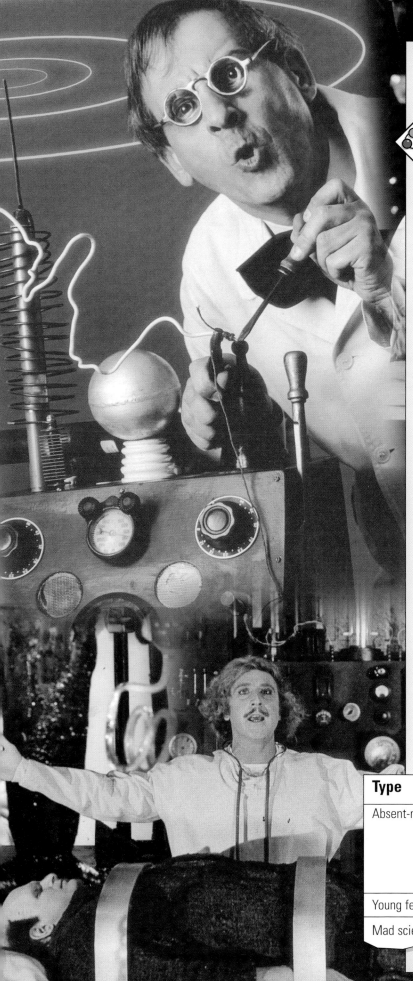

1. Draw a sketch of what you think a scientist looks like. Don't worry about your ability as an artist; the sketch doesn't have to be a masterpiece. Do not sign your picture. Some of the pictures will be posted by your teacher.

2. How do you view scientists? Do they work alone? Do they have interests beyond science? In general, do you believe scientists are concerned with politics? sports? money? fashion?

3. Working in a small group, survey the pictures drawn by your class.

   a) See if you can pick out some characteristics that are common in the pictures. Are the scientists generally young, or old? Are they mostly male, or female? Are their clothes modern, or old-fashioned? What other characteristics do they seem to have?

   b) How does each characteristic affect the way we view scientists?

4. In books, movies, and on television, scientists seem to come in types. Brainstorm a list of types of scientists that you have seen or read about, and make a list of characteristics for each type. Make your list into a table, like the one below.

| Type | Characteristics |
|---|---|
| Absent-minded professor | • forgetful<br>• shy, modest<br>• not interested in the material things in life... |
| Young female scientist | |
| Mad scientist | |

# Scientific Problem Solving

- What do scientists do?
- How do they go about making discoveries?
- What is a scientific question?
- Are there some questions that scientists can't answer?
- Who decides whether scientists' interpretations are correct?
- How does science affect your life?

These are a few questions that deal with the nature of science. Science is about asking questions, gathering evidence, proposing solutions, and testing the solutions. In this unit, you will explore science as an approach to solving problems and making sense of our natural world. Scientists often construct **theories** to explain what they have observed. Because these theories rely on experimental evidence, it is not unusual for the theories to change as more evidence is gathered.

## From Observation to Theory

Alfred Wegener once looked at a map and noticed how the shores of different continents appear to fit together. He wondered whether it was possible that Africa and South America were once connected. In 1912, Wegener suggested that land masses were not fixed in position but floated over the planet on a sea of molten rock.

At first, Wegener's idea of continental drift was met with doubt by other scientists. Just proposing a novel **hypothesis** is not enough to convince most scientists. They need evidence. Wegener began looking for evidence to support his hypothesis.

Both Europe and North America have wolves.

Wegener's Biological Evidence

Animals in several continents seem very similar.

African dromedaries and South American llamas seem very much like each other.

The American jaguar and the African leopard seem related.

Freshwater pike are very similar in Europe and North America. Because these animals die after a short time in salt water, it is highly unlikely that they swam from one continent to the other.

## The Theory

From Wegener's ideas, his evidence, and the evidence collected by many other scientists, the theory of plate tectonics was developed. With this theory, more of what happens on Earth can be explained. The formation of mountains can be explained by the crushing movement of plates that strike each other. Even earthquakes and volcanoes are more easily understood by using the theory of plate tectonics.

## Scientific Problem Solving

The construction of Wegener's theory of continental drift allows us to understand how scientists go about problem-solving. The model below provides an outline for scientific problem-solving.

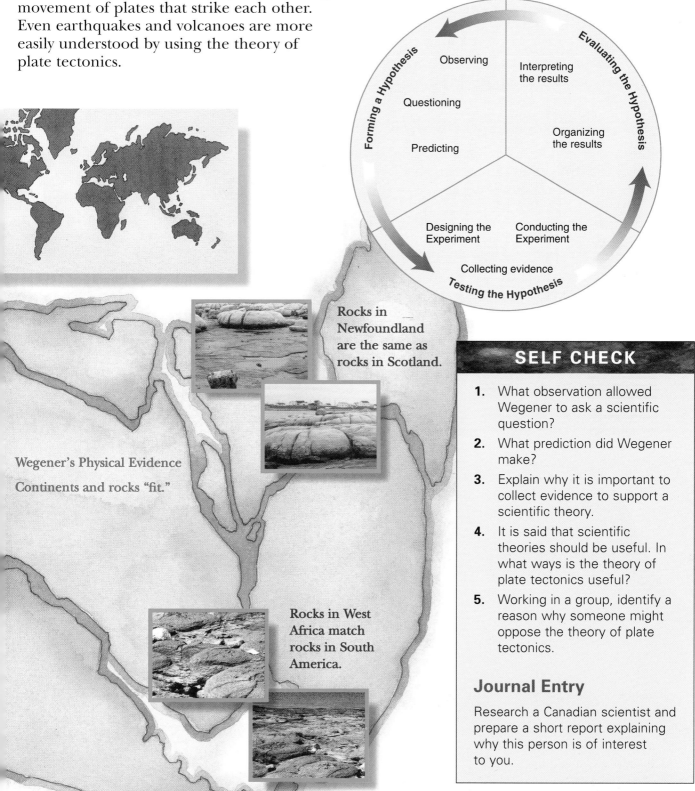

Forming a Hypothesis
- Observing
- Questioning
- Predicting

Evaluating the Hypothesis
- Interpreting the results
- Organizing the results

Testing the Hypothesis
- Designing the Experiment
- Conducting the Experiment
- Collecting evidence

Rocks in Newfoundland are the same as rocks in Scotland.

Wegener's Physical Evidence
Continents and rocks "fit."

Rocks in West Africa match rocks in South America.

### SELF CHECK

1. What observation allowed Wegener to ask a scientific question?

2. What prediction did Wegener make?

3. Explain why it is important to collect evidence to support a scientific theory.

4. It is said that scientific theories should be useful. In what ways is the theory of plate tectonics useful?

5. Working in a group, identify a reason why someone might oppose the theory of plate tectonics.

### Journal Entry

Research a Canadian scientist and prepare a short report explaining why this person is of interest to you.

# Constructing Scientific Questions

THE MODEL OF SCIENTIFIC PROBLEM-SOLVING often begins with forming a **scientific question**. Careful observation leads to scientific questions. Questions allow the scientist to make predictions about what will happen in similar situations. Unlike other predictions, predictions that come from scientific questions can be tested by doing experiments. If the prediction is supported by the experiment, the scientist will often attempt an explanation. In this investigation, you will gain practice in forming scientific questions about temperature and heat. The scientific questions will require you to make predictions about similar events and offer an explanation.

## Materials

- safety glasses
- apron
- thermometer
- 3 small test tubes
- test-tube rack
- medicine dropper
- heat liniment
- rubbing alcohol
- water
- tennis ball
- metre stick

## Procedure

1 Ask your laboratory partner to look away.
   ■ Using a medicine dropper, place a single drop of water, rubbing alcohol, and heat liniment onto the inside of your laboratory partner's arm at three separate spots.
   ■ Rinse the medicine dropper after each transfer.
   ■ After one minute, use a paper towel to wash the liquids from your laboratory partner's arm.

   a) Could your laboratory partner detect if any of the drops felt warm, or cool?

   b) Suggest why safety glasses are worn for this activity.

   c) You will test water, alcohol, and heat liniment with a thermometer. Make a prediction about which is warmest and which is coldest.

   **Caution: Heat liniment is toxic if swallowed.**

*Observation: Chili peppers taste hot, and wintergreen and mint feel cool.*

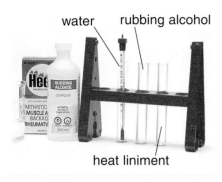

water    rubbing alcohol

heat liniment

**2** Place 10 drops of water, rubbing alcohol, and heat liniment into three small test tubes.

■ Rinse the medicine dropper after each substance is used.

■ Place a thermometer in each test tube for one minute and record the temperature.

■ Remember to rinse the thermometer after putting it in each test tube.

✎ d) What question is being investigated by this experiment?

✎ e) What evidence is being gathered to answer the question?

Wash your hands with soap and water.

*Observation: Have you ever kicked a ball during the winter? It almost feels like kicking a brick.*

**3** A tennis ball has been kept in a refrigerator overnight.

■ Hold a metre stick vertically with the zero end on the floor.

■ Drop the cold tennis ball from the upper end of the metre stick.

■ Measure the height that the tennis ball bounces back.

■ Do this three times (each time is called a trial).

**4** Repeat step 3 with a ball that is at room temperature.

✎ f) What question is being investigated by this experiment?

✎ g) What evidence is being gathered to answer the question?

✎ h) Why are three different trials used?

---

## Investigation Questions

1. Is it possible for a food to feel hot in your mouth, but not hot to touch? Provide an example.

2. In 1965, a strange argument occurred during a weekend baseball game between the Detroit Tigers and the Chicago White Sox. The White Sox were accused of cooling the baseballs. In five games, only 17 runs were scored in Chicago, while these same two teams registered 59 runs in Detroit.

   a) Construct a scientific question from this observation.

   b) Suggest a procedure for testing this question.

3. Look around your classroom and make an observation. State a scientific question that could be asked from your observation.

## Extension

4. Rub the tennis ball vigorously along the surface of a table for 30 s. Now repeat the procedure you used in steps 3 and 4 for bouncing the ball.

   a) How does rubbing the ball along the table surface affect the way the ball bounces?

   b) A scientist observes that a tennis ball bounces differently at the end of a game than it did at the beginning of the game. Construct a scientific question from this observation.

   c) Suggest a procedure that would allow you to test this question.

# Science at the Scene of an Accident

THE POWER OF OBSERVATION is the best tool that both a detective and a scientist have. Observations include details that may or may not be important. A detective calls these clues. A scientist calls them data. Later, both the detective and the scientist will use this information to make conclusions about what has happened. How good are your skills of observation? Try this activity to find out.

## Procedure

**1** Look at the picture on these pages for exactly three minutes. Close the book.

**2** Draw a sketch of what you remember of the scene and list as many observations as you can.

**3** Turn to page 47 and answer the questions. Put a check next to each observation on your list that answered a question.

**4** After you have tried to answer as many questions as you can, form a small group and share your answers.

**5** Review your answers by looking at the picture again.

# Using Your Senses

**B**ESIDES DIRECTLY SEEING AN OBJECT, scientists have other ways to observe an experiment. They are trained to use all their senses. This investigation will let you test your own ability to use some of your senses.

All of your senses can give you valuable information.

## Materials

- shoe box
- various items— wood block, rubber stopper, plastic straw, metal jar lid, piece of fruit such as an apple, a bar of soap, etc.
- masking tape
- marble

## Procedure

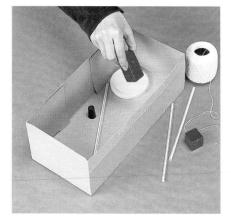

**1** Select several items and place them in the box.
  - Tape the items in place.
  - Remove all other items.

**2** Place the marble in the box.
  - Replace the lid and tape it closed.
  - Trade boxes with someone else in class.

**3** Without opening the box, try to figure out how many objects are in the box, what they are made of, and where they are located.

1. Compare your predictions with what were actually in the box. Which objects were the most difficult to identify? Which objects were the easiest to identify? Why?

2. Which senses did you use most in this investigation? Which senses did you use least?

## Apply

3. Give one example each of how the senses of smell, touch, and hearing could be useful in a science experiment.

4. Why might it be dangerous sometimes to use your senses while performing a science experiment? Give an example for each sense.

## Extension

5. Over the years, scientists have made several models of how the sun and the planets in our solar system move. Their observations led first to the conclusion that the Sun and planets moved in circles around the Earth. Later, they concluded that the planets, including Earth, moved around the Sun. What limits do our observations have in making models in science?

Early model of solar system

Recent model of solar system

a) List the observations that you make, and any guesses about what each observation means.

b) Based on your guesses, make a map of the inside of the box, indicating where all the objects are, and what they are.

4 Open the box.

c) Make a map showing the objects in the box.

# Mapping the Ocean's Floor

**A**S YOU HAVE DISCOVERED, scientists often have to observe things that they cannot see. One place that happens is in the ocean. How do scientists map the ocean floor when they can't see it? In this activity, you'll learn one way this can be done.

## Materials

- shoe box
- newspaper
- papier maché
- pencil
- ruler
- butcher paper
- tape
- marking pen
- clear plastic drinking straw
- string
- scissors
- small fishing weight

## Procedure

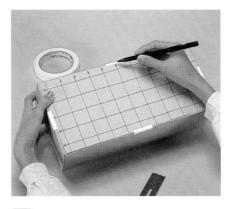

**1** Make an ocean floor.
■ Wad several pieces of newspaper and place them in the bottom of the box.
■ Use the papier maché to cover the wads, creating an uneven surface at the bottom of the box.
■ Allow to dry.

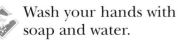 Wash your hands with soap and water.

**2** Make the surface of the ocean.
■ On a piece of butcher paper, draw 3 cm × 3 cm grid lines.
■ Cut out a piece of paper large enough to cover the top of the box.
■ Tape the paper to the top of the box.
■ Number or letter each line on the grid so all of the intersections have coordinates.
■ Use a pencil to make a hole at each intersection.

**3** Make your measuring device.
■ Thread the string through the straw and tie the fishing weight to the end.
■ Tape the straw to the ruler so that when the weight is pulled up to the straw, the bottom of the weight is flush with the bottom end of the ruler.
■ Draw an ink mark on the string at the other end of the ruler.

A map of the floor of the Pacific Ocean. Scientists have mapped the floors of all the oceans, without once standing on the bottom.

## Investigation Questions

1. How accurately were you able to map the surface at the bottom of the box? Were you able to discover all the high and low points?

2. What problems did you experience in this investigation? How could you improve the procedure to eliminate the problems?

## Apply

3. How could marine scientists use similar methods to map the ocean floor? What other techniques could they use?

4. Look up the word "sonar". How could sonar be used to map the ocean floor?

## Extension

5. Cover your box and exchange boxes with another team. Repeat the measuring and mapping process. Can you accurately determine the ocean floor for their box?

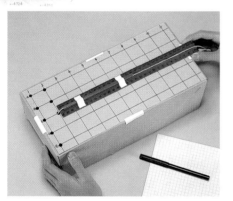

**4** Start measuring depths.
■ For each hole in the paper, pull the string so the ink mark is at the end of the ruler.
■ Place your device over the hole and lower the weight until it touches the surface at the bottom.

a) Record the coordinates of the hole, and how far down the ruler your mark is.

**5** Mark a piece of graph paper with the same grid you used for the ocean surface.
■ Put in the "depth" at each point.
■ Connect points that have the same depth and that are next to each other with a line.
■ The lines connecting equal points are called isolines. Together they will show a profile of your ocean floor.

b) Label any identifiable features, such as trenches, mountains, etc.

c) Remove the paper from the box. Compare your profile with the actual bottom. How close were you?

# Forensic Dentist

S CIENCE CAN BE USED in many careers. For example, you might expect that a dentist would have to know science to do the job properly. But did you know that a dentist can be a scientist too?

Meet David Sweet. David teaches dentistry at the University of British Columbia's School of Dentistry. But he is also a forensic dentist, a consultant for the RCMP's crime lab unit. On a normal day, David may start by teaching a group of first-year dentistry students the anatomy of the mouth and watch over second-year students in the school's dental clinic. In the afternoon, he might get a call from a police inspector, asking how to preserve and collect dental evidence at the scene of a crime.

In some serious cases, David may be asked to fly across the country for a forensic investigation or to act as an expert witness in a trial.

And what does David do in his spare time? He goes to school. He just received his Ph.D. after researching how to extract DNA from saliva samples. He has shown that a suspect's DNA can even be matched to saliva found on a piece of chewed gum left at a crime scene!

David continually looks for new ways to analyze evidence using the same activities that all scientists do: observation, classification, comparison, measuring, predicting, interpreting data, and drawing reasonable conclusions.

## Making Impressions

Forensic dentists use impressions of teeth to help in identification. Try this activity and become a forensic dentist. You will need rubber gloves, scissors, a styrofoam plate, a marking pen, and a magnifying glass.

**Caution: Wear rubber gloves while doing this activity.**

- Cut a styrofoam plate in half. Stack the two halves together, then cut the halves into thirds. You should now have six wedge-shaped pieces. Flatten the pointed ends of the wedges by cutting about 3 cm from the tip.

- Slip the cut ends of two stacked wedges into your mouth. Push them in as far as possible while still being comfortable.

- Bite down on the wedges firmly, then remove them. Label the top wedge "Impression of the Top Teeth" and the bottom wedge "Impression of the Bottom Teeth".

- Have your teacher dip the impressions in bleach.

- Examine your teeth impressions.

a) How many teeth marks are in the top impression? How many are on the bottom impression?

b) How are the teeth impressions from the top different from the impressions on the bottom? How are they the same?

- Examine the teeth impressions of other students.

c) How are their teeth impressions similar to yours? How are they different?

d) What features of your teeth would be most useful to identify yours?

e) Why do you think the impressions were dipped in bleach?

# Working Safely in the Laboratory

ALTHOUGH ALL OF THE activities you do in the laboratory have been selected with your safety in mind, the laboratory must still be regarded as a serious workplace. In this case study, you will work in small groups to learn about hazardous chemicals. Later you will be asked to identify potentially unsafe procedures.

Become familiar with the warning symbols that are placed on potentially dangerous materials. You should be able to identify and understand each of the symbols shown here.

## Hazardous Household Product Symbols

The warning symbols on household products were developed to indicate exactly why and to what degree a product is dangerous.

## WHMIS Symbols

The Workplace Hazardous Materials Information System (WHMIS) symbols were developed to standardize the labelling of dangerous materials used in all workplaces, including schools. Pay careful attention to any warning symbols on the products or materials that you handle.

## Working Safely with Chemicals

**Caution: We recommend wearing safety goggles, rubber gloves, and an apron to work with all chemicals.**

Each laboratory group will be given three different chemicals commonly found in the laboratory or home. Without opening the containers, study the symbols on the bottles.

a) Identify each chemical or household product and list the caution symbols you find on each container.

b) Make a list of rules for handling each chemical. The following questions may help in making the list.

- What would you do if you spilled this chemical?
- Should you wear protective glasses and a laboratory apron while handling it?
- Would a nearby open flame present problems?
- Is it a good idea to use this chemical in an enclosed space?
- Would it be dangerous to store this chemical in a warm location?
- Where would you store it?

## Finding a Better Way

Examine the pictures on this page and identify procedures that you believe could cause a problem.

c) Make a list of things that you think are not safe in each of the pictures. Explain why you believe the procedure is unsafe.

d) How would you change what is happening in each of the pictures to make it safe?

### Case Study Questions

1. In a group, work to create a list of safety procedures for all experiments. Your teacher will help you compile the list into a set of rules for the class.

2. Why is it unacceptable to ever taste a solution in the laboratory?

3. Briefly describe the procedure you would follow if your skin comes in contact with an unknown chemical.

4. Why is it important to have a separate container for the disposal of broken glass?

5. Why are sandals and other open-toed shoes not recommended in the laboratory?

### Extension

6. Draw a map of the route your class should follow when the fire alarm sounds.

7. Draw a map of where the safety materials are in your classroom.

# Testing Predictions

**I**N THIS ACTIVITY, you will gain experience in making predictions. Like scientists, you will develop procedures and design equipment that will check your predictions.

## Materials

- ruler
- blank paper
- scissors
- protractor
- modelling clay
- jar with screw-top lid
- plank (inclined plane)
- books

## Procedure

*Why Do We Test Predictions?*

**1** View the diagram above.

a) Do the white areas have parallel sides? Make a prediction.

b) Describe a technique that will allow you to determine whether the white areas are true squares.

**2** Stare intensely at the grid above for 20 s.

c) Do you see grey dots at the corners of the green grid squares?

d) Describe a technique that will allow you to determine if the grey dots are actually present.

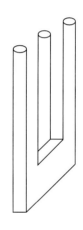

**3** View the diagram above. How many pillars do you see? Try building the object using modelling clay.

e) Did you have any difficulties building your model?

## Making and Testing Predictions

**4** Support a plank with some books, so it forms an inclined plane. When you roll a jar down the plane, which will roll farther: an empty jar, or one filled with water? Make a prediction, then carry out the experiment.

✎ f) How accurate was your prediction?

✎ g) Provide a theory, or explanation, that accounts for your observations.

**5** Now empty half of the water from the jar. How far will it roll? Make a prediction about how far the jar will travel, and try the experiment.

### Investigation Questions

1. Why is it important to test predictions?

2. In step 3, you constructed a model to test your prediction. Explain how the model helped you understand the diagram.

3. Scientists will change their theories if they don't result in accurate predictions. Explain how step 5 provides support for this statement.

### Extension

4. Will a jar that is one-quarter full travel farther or less far than one that is half-full? How about a jar that is three-quarters full? Make your predictions and test them.

5. Will the type of fluid in the jar affect the distance the jar rolls? Try vegetable oil. Make your predictions and test them.

# Forming a Scientific Hypothesis

WHEN YOU ROLLED THE JARS DOWN the plane, you gained experience making predictions. A scientific prediction must include a cause-and-effect relationship. Here's an example of a cause-and-effect relationship: the more water in the jar, the farther the jar will roll. The amount of water (cause) affects the distance the jar rolls (effect).

## What Is a Hypothesis?

When a prediction can be tested by experiment it is said to be a **hypothesis.** Scientists often use hypotheses (plural of hypothesis) because they lead to conclusions.

Hypotheses are often stated in the "if ... then" format. For example, you learned that a jar filled with water rolled farther than an empty one after moving down an inclined plane. You could write the hypothesis this way:

*If* a jar has a greater mass, *then* it will roll farther after it leaves a ramp.

The hypothesis includes a cause (the mass of the jar) and an effect (the distance the jar rolls). This hypothesis allows you to make predictions about other situations. Based on this hypothesis, you might predict that a half-full jar will roll farther than an empty one, but not as far as a full one. Unfortunately, this wonderful prediction does not stand up to testing. Something is wrong with the hypothesis: there must be some factors at work other than just the mass.

The angle of the ramp is an independent variable.

## What are Variables?

The mass of the jar and the distance that it rolls are called variables. Anything that can cause a change is a **variable.** Any variable that can be changed by the experimenter is called an **independent variable.** For example, the mass of the jar is an independent variable: the experimenter can add or remove water.

The effect of the change is called the **dependent variable.** The distance that the jar travels is the dependent variable.

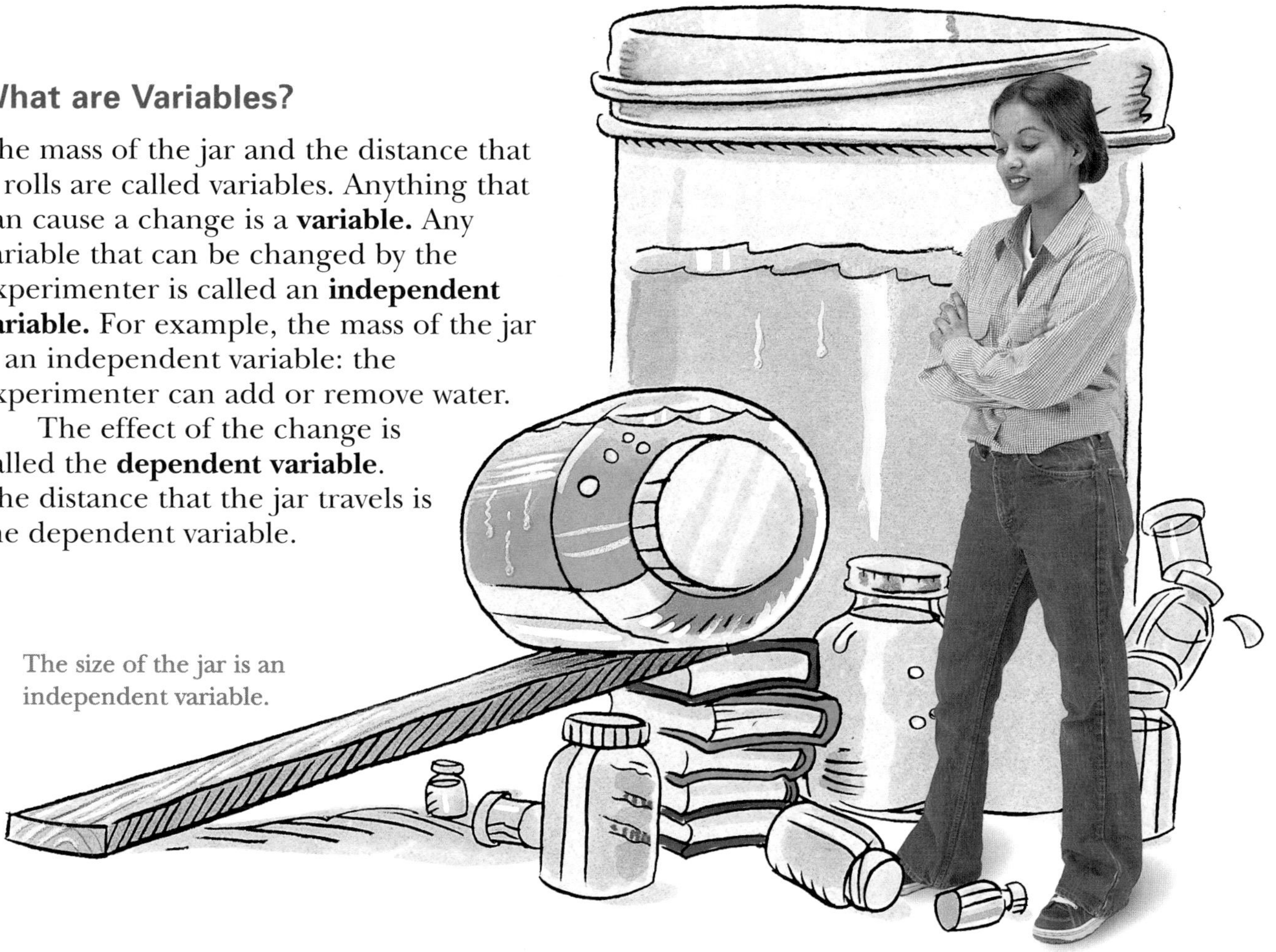

The size of the jar is an independent variable.

The type of liquid in the jar is an independent variable.

HIGH-GRADE INDUSTRIAL KETCHUP

PAINT

MUSTARD

Maple Syrup

The empty jar on the ramp is a control.

## What Is a Control?

Scientists attempt to test only one independent variable at a time. That way the scientist knows which cause produced the effect. **Controls** are used to eliminate the possibility of an unknown variable.

Remember how the jar half-filled with water surprised you? As this jar rolled down the ramp, water sloshed back and forth, creating friction. The friction inside the jar slowed it down, and it didn't travel as far. The jar with no water in it wasn't affected by this variable: it was the control.

## Why Do Scientists Use Controls?

The following experiment shows why scientists use a control. A student notices spots of rust on the frame of her bike after riding all winter. The student hypothesizes that the rust was caused by the salt on the roads. But is salt the only variable? It is possible that the rusting was not caused by the salt alone. For example, the roads were also wet a lot of the winter. By comparing the amount of rusting with and without salt, you can determine just how much rusting is caused by the salt.

**OBSERVATION:**
You notice patches of rust on your bike after a winter of riding it to school.

↓

**QUESTION:**
Is the salt on the roads causing the rusting?

↓

**HYPOTHESIS:**
If metal is exposed to salt, then rusting will occur.

24

## TRY THIS

### Salt and Corrosion

Does road salt cause rusting? Is there a better type of salt for use on roads? You will be given three different types of salt (sodium chloride, potassium chloride, and calcium chloride). Use steel wool for the metal.

- State your hypothesis.
- Identify your variables.
- Make a prediction.
- Design an experiment to test your hypothesis. Include a control.
- Present your procedure to your teacher for approval before beginning.
- Gather equipment and begin the experiment.
- Present your observations.
- Draw a conclusion. Did your observations support your hypothesis?

## SELF CHECK

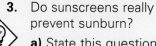

1. What is a hypothesis?
2. A student observes that milk has a different taste if it is left out on the table for more than three hours. List the variables, other than the time that it has been left on the table, that might affect taste.
3. Do sunscreens really prevent sunburn?
   a) State this question as a hypothesis.
   b) Suggest an experimental design that would test your hypothesis.
   c) Identify the dependent and independent variables in your experiment.
   d) What would you use as a control?

The Experiment:
Metal placed in different solutions

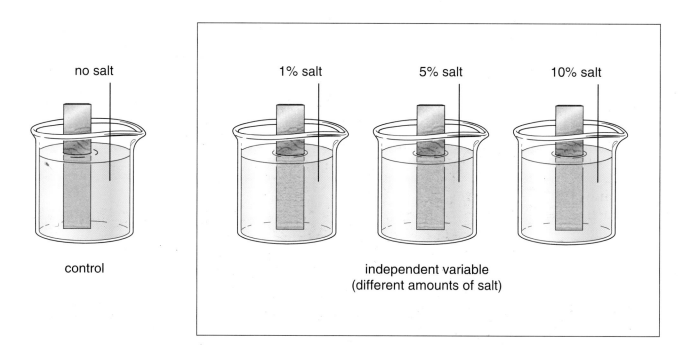

no salt

1% salt

5% salt

10% salt

control

independent variable
(different amounts of salt)

# *Thinking Like a Scientist*

A SCIENTIST WILL OFTEN ORGANIZE AN EXPERIMENT to make it easier to do and to understand. In this investigation, you will think and act like a scientist as you study the factors (variables) that affect the swing time of a pendulum. In any experiment, a scientist wants to control the variables so that only one of them is tested at a time. In this investigation, you will test several variables that might affect the number of swings a pendulum makes. Each variable will be tested separately, and the others will be controlled.

## Materials

- string
- paper clips
- metal washers
- pencils
- timing device
- cardboard
- hooks

## Procedure

*Part 1: How Does a Pendulum Swing?*

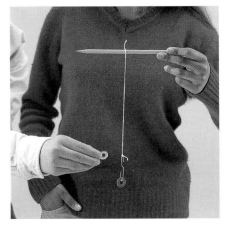

**1** Make a pendulum by taking a piece of string and making loops at each end.
- Hook one loop over a pencil.
- Open a paper clip to make a hook and place it on the other loop.
- Place a couple of washers on the hook.

**2** Keeping the pencil still, let your pendulum swing gently.
- Measure the number of swings your pendulum makes in 15 s. (One swing is when the washers move away from you and back to their starting point.)

a) Record the number of swings.

b) Compare your results with those of other students in the class. Did all students get the same number of swings?

c) Why do you think your classmates got different results?

d) The factors that affect the outcome of your experiment are called variables. Make a list of variables that might affect the number of swings of a pendulum.

*Part 2: Does Mass Affect the Swing of a Pendulum?*

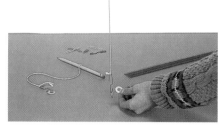

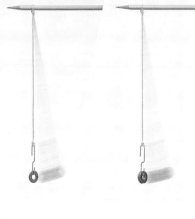

**3** Make two pendulums that are 30 cm long, including the loops. Place one washer on one pendulum and two washers on the other. Predict which washer will make the most swings in 15 s.

✎ e) Record your prediction.

**4** Pull the washer on the first pendulum until the string makes a 45° angle with the vertical. Release the washer and count the number of swings it makes in 15 s.
  ■ Repeat with the second pendulum.

✎ f) Record your results.

✎ g) Was your prediction correct? Does the mass affect the number of swings?

*Part 3: Does Arc Length Affect the Swing of a Pendulum?*

**5** Use the pendulum with one washer from step 4. Predict how the size of the angle the washer is pulled out (the arc length) will affect the number of swings in 15 s.

🖎 h) Record your prediction.

**6** Holding the pencil, pull the washer out until the string makes a 45° angle. Release the washer and count the number of swings in 15 s. Repeat the experiment, this time using a 90° angle.

🖎 i) Record your results.

🖎 j) Was your prediction correct? Does arc length affect the number of swings?

*Part 5: Graphing the Results*
*You should have an idea of which variables affect the number of swings the pendulum makes in 15 seconds. One way to represent the results of your data is through a graph. When you have many pieces of data, a graph can give you a visual representation of the data.*

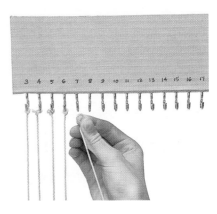

**9** Your class will need a strip of cardboard with the numbers 3 to 20 spaced evenly along its length. Insert a hook into the cardboard below each number.

**10** Each group will make two more pendulums, each with a different length of string. Make one pendulum shorter than 30 cm and one longer than 45 cm. Using the same procedure as in Part 4, count the number of swings your pendulums make in 15 s.

🖎 n) Record the number of swings of each pendulum.

**11** Hang your pendulums on the cardboard strip. Put them on the hook under the number of swings they make in 15 s. The rest of the class will do the same.

🖎 o) What do you notice about the shape the pendulum strings make when all the pendulums from the class are on the hooks?

*Part 4: Does the Length of the Pendulum's String Affect the Swing?*

**7** Make another pendulum, 45 cm long with one washer. Based on this pendulum and the 30-cm one in Part 3, predict which pendulum will swing more in 15 s.

  k) Record your prediction.

**8** Pull the washer of the 30-cm pendulum out until the string makes a 45° angle. Release the washer and count the number of swings in 15 s. Repeat with the 45-cm pendulum.

  l) Record your results.

  m) Was your prediction correct? Does the length of the pendulum string affect the number of swings?

## Investigation Questions

1. What variables affect the number of swings that a pendulum makes in 15 s?

2. What variables do not affect the number of swings that a pendulum makes in 15 s?

3. Look at the board where the class has hung its pendulums. Are there numbers with more than one pendulum attached? If so, what do you notice about the length of those pendulums?

4. What variables were controlled in Part 2? How were they controlled? Which variable was tested?

5. What variables were controlled in Part 3? How were they controlled? Which variable was tested?

6. What variables were controlled in Part 4? How were they controlled? Which variable was tested?

## Apply

7. List places where you have seen pendulums outside of the classroom. What was their purpose?

## Extension

8. Pendulums are often used as part of a timing device, like a grandfather clock. Design a pendulum timing device that is an accurate way to measure one minute. Submit your design to your teacher for approval, then make the pendulum. Test the pendulum to see how accurate it is. Record your data and state your conclusion.

# Organizing Scientific Investigations

THERE ARE SEVERAL WAYS TO ORGANIZE a scientific experiment. One way is to use the problem-solving or inquiry model. The problem-solving model has several steps and may also be used to solve problems in other areas, such as mathematics and technology. The steps in this model are given below:

1
- Pose or define the question: Determine what you are trying to find out.

2
- Develop a hypothesis: Propose an answer to the question.
  a) What do you think will happen?
  b) What are your reasons for this prediction?

4
- Conduct the experiment: Test your hypothesis.
  a) Collect and record data from the experiment.
  b) Organize the data using charts, graphs, etc.

3
- Think of an experiment that may reveal what you want to know: Decide on your procedure.
  a) What steps will you follow as you do the experiment?
  b) What safety precautions will you follow?
  c) Will you need a control?
  d) Make a list of materials needed for the experiment.
  e) Decide how you will obtain your data.
  f) Decide how you will record and organize your data.

5
- Draw conclusions from the observations: Confirm or revise the hypothesis.
  a) Do the data agree with your prediction? Suggest why or why not. Does your hypothesis need to be changed?
  b) Do you need more data? If so, suggest another experiment you could do.

6
- Communicate your findings.

### Tying up Loose Ends

Scientists check each other's work by repeating their colleagues' procedures, to discover if they get the same results. To make sure there is no misunderstanding, procedures have to be written up clearly. This is not as easy as it may sound.

Try this:

- Write down the steps necessary to tie your shoes.
- Give the steps to another student.
- The other student will carry out the instructions precisely as written.

a) How good was your procedure? Could the other student tie her or his shoes following only your procedure?

b) What additional steps could you add that would make your procedure clear?

## SELF CHECK

1. Why do you think there are standard methods for scientific investigations?

2. At one time, most people believed that the world was flat. What observations would lead to that conclusion? Name another generally held belief that has changed because of changing scientific explanations.

3. Decide on a hypothesis and design an experiment that investigates the question, "Do plants need sunlight in order to grow well?"

4. Decide on a hypothesis and design an experiment that investigates the question, "Do Brand X or Brand Y tennis balls bounce better?"

### Extension

5. Submit your experimental design for questions 3 or 4, or another of your choice, to your teacher for approval, then do the experiment. Record your data and state your conclusion.

6. Apply the problem-solving model to a problem in technology, such as, "How can I design a container for an egg so it can fall from a given height without breaking?"

# Experimental Design

A television commercial states that a certain laundry detergent gets clothes the whitest. Is the manufacturer's claim correct?

YOU'VE HAD A CHANCE TO PERFORM several scientific experiments and design others in this unit. Now it's your chance to design and perform a scientific experiment to discover something that you may have wondered about.

On these pages, you will find some questions to start you off, or you can investigate your own question.

**CAUTION: Be sure to submit your experimental design to your teacher for approval before you do the experiment. Your design should include safety precautions.**

"NOTHING'S WHITER THAN SLICK!"

## Procedure

**1** Remember all you have learned about how to organize a science experiment. When designing an experiment remember to:

- Decide what question your experiment will investigate.

- Develop a hypothesis to answer your question.

- Design an experiment that tests your hypothesis.

- Draw conclusions from the observations you make.

- Confirm or revise the hypothesis.

- Communicate your findings.

A home gardener is growing several geraniums indoors for transplanting in the spring. The plants are beginning to wither and die. One member of the family suggests that the geraniums are receiving too much water; another member thinks they are receiving too little. Who is correct?

You may have heard that hot tap water makes ice cubes faster than cold tap water. Is it true?

A friend tells you that wearing nail polish makes fingernails long and strong. Is this true?

Which paper towels really absorb the most water?

A cook adds salt to water to make it boil at a higher temperature. Will this work? If it does, how much salt is necessary?

## Investigation Questions

1. Commercials often give the impression that a scientific experiment has been done to test the product. Make a list of statements that might give that impression.

## Extension

2. What kinds of people are shown in advertising? As you watch television or read the newspaper, make a note of the product in each ad, and the principal person in the ad. What kind of product is being advertised? Is the person male or female? What age is the person? What ethnic group does the person belong to? Write a report on your research.

# Evaluating Experimental Designs

HAVE YOU EVER NOTICED THAT roads and sidewalks are salted during the winter? Does the salt cause the temperature to increase? What is the best type of salt? A group of students investigated these questions. They proposed two hypotheses and designed two different procedures to test each hypothesis. Both of the experimental designs contain errors. Your challenge is to follow the students' procedures, identify the design errors, and then to correct them.

## Materials

- safety goggles
- apron
- styrofoam cup
- thermometer
- sodium chloride
- graduated cylinder
- teaspoon (or triple-beam balance)
- zip-lock plastic bag
- calcium chloride
- potassium chloride
- kitty litter
- ice cubes
- permanent marker

Have you ever seen salt being spread on a sidewalk or road? Some people insist that kitty litter works better than salt.

## Procedure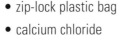

*Part 1: Does Salt Increase the Temperature of Ice Water?*
*Hypothesis 1: If salt is added to ice water, then the temperature of the ice water increases.*

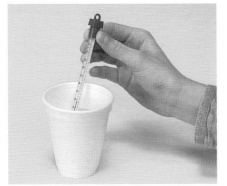

**1** Place two ice cubes in a styrofoam cup.
  - Using a graduated cylinder, add 25 mL of cold tap water.
  - Use a thermometer to take the temperature of the water.

 a) Record the temperature of the water.

**2** Add one level teaspoon of sodium chloride to the solution. (If a triple-beam balance is available, you can weigh 5 g of salt.)
  - Wait 5 min and then once again take the temperature.

 b) Record the new temperature of the water.

**3** Evaluate part 1.

 c) Identify sources of error in this procedure. (Did the procedure test Hypothesis 1?)

 d) Present your redesigned procedure to your teacher, redo the experiment, and present your results.

 **Caution: Handle all chemicals with care. If chemicals come in contact with your skin, rinse the area well with cold water and inform your teacher.**

**Investigation Questions**

1. For Part 1, identify the following in your revised design:

   **a)** independent variable

   **b)** dependent variable

   **c)** control

2. For Part 2, identify the following in your revised design:

   **a)** independent variable

   **b)** dependent variable

   **c)** control

3. If you were to go into business making a product that removed ice from sidewalks, what factors other than amount of melting would you have to consider?

**Extension**

4. Determine the amount of melting that occurred at 5-min intervals for each of the different types of salt. Express your data in the form of a graph.

*Part 2: Which Type of Salt is Best for Removing Ice?*
*Hypothesis 2: If kitty litter is added to ice, then it will cause more melting than salts.*

**6** Evaluate Part 2.

✎ f) Identify sources of error in this procedure. (Did the procedure test Hypothesis 2?)

✎ g) Present your redesigned procedure to your teacher, redo the experiment, and present your results.

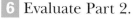 Wash your hands with soap and water.

**4** Place ice in four bags.
   ■ Add a level teaspoon of calcium chloride to bag 1, a heaping teaspoon of potassium chloride to bag 2, two level teaspoons of sodium chloride to bag 3, and two heaping teaspoons of kitty litter to bag 4. Allow each to sit in a warm or sunny place for 5 min.

**5** Open the plastic bag and pour the liquid contents into a graduated cylinder. How much melting occurred in each of the bags?

✎ e) Record the amount of liquid poured from each bag.

INVESTIGATION

# Technological Problem Solving

**S**CIENCE EXPLAINS HOW THE NATURAL WORLD WORKS. Technology changes the world. Most often, technological devices are designed to improve our lives. For a technological solution to work, the cost, efficiency, and environmental impact of the solution must be considered.

In this investigation, your group will be assigned a technological problem. To solve the problem, you will use a modelling experiment. **Models** are used as small-scale tests for larger, more expensive future experiments. Cheap models also allow a trial-and-error approach that would be far too expensive for full-scale tests.

In Part 1, your group will compete against other design groups to create the barge capable of carrying the greatest number of marbles. In Part 2, your group will design a device to move objects along an assembly line.

## Materials

Part 1:
- large ice cream bucket
- 250 g of modelling clay
- marbles

## Procedure

*Part 1: Designing a Barge*

**1** Working with all the members of your group, create a diagram for the barge's design. Build your barge using only the modelling clay you have been given.

**2** Fill an ice cream bucket with water and place your barge on the surface of the water. Begin adding marbles until the barge begins to sink.

✏ a) Record the maximum number of marbles that could be added.

## Materials

Part 2:
- 10 popsicle sticks or 10 soda straws
- 3 ping-pong balls
- 2 250-mL beakers
- 10 thumb tacks
- 1 m of masking tape
- stop watch or a watch with a second hand

*Part 2: Designing an Automated Assembly Line*

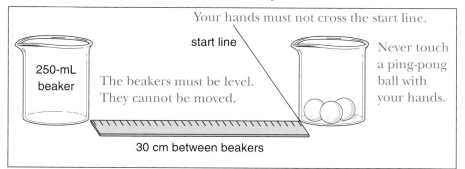

Your hands must not cross the start line.

start line

250-mL beaker

The beakers must be level. They cannot be moved.

Never touch a ping-pong ball with your hands.

30 cm between beakers

**3** Draw a diagram of the device that your group intends to build. The device must move three ping-pong balls from one beaker to another in the shortest time possible.

 b) Explain why your group chose the design features it did.

**4** Build the device and test it a few times before asking a judge to begin timing the delivery of the ping-pong balls between beakers.

c) How long did it take to deliver all three ping-pong balls?

## Investigation Questions

1. Identify one advantage of using models when solving technological problems.

2. Examine the class designs for Part 1 or Part 2 of the experiment. Which group had the best design? What design features made it superior?

3. Explain how you would change the design you used, if you were to make another model.

## Apply

4. Give three examples of problems that technology can solve.

5. If you were designing a barge, what factors other than its ability to carry heavy cargo must be considered in the design? Give your reasons.

# Was it Good Science, or an Accident?

I T IS DIFFICULT TO IMAGINE THAT a mold like the ones in the photographs can provide a substance that helps to control disease. But that is exactly what it does. Since it was first used about 50 years ago, an antibiotic from a mold similar to this has cured millions of people. (Antibiotics kill bacteria.)

The antibiotic is penicillin—and it was discovered by accident.

a) How could you determine if a substance could be used to kill bacteria?

b) What problems do you think scientists face when they work with chemical cures used with humans?

## Alexander Fleming

The discoverer of penicillin, Alexander Fleming, was born in Scotland in 1881. After finishing medical school, he became interested in finding ways to kill the bacteria that cause diseases in humans. At that time, many of the chemicals that killed bacteria also killed healthy body cells.

During World War I, Dr. Fleming carried out research on how wounds healed. He showed that white blood cells helped to fight infections caused by bacteria in wounds.

c) What did Dr. Fleming do that made him both a doctor and a scientist?

## The Discovery

In the years following this and other discoveries, Dr. Fleming continued to look for a chemical that would be effective in combatting bacteria, but would not harm the human body. In order to test various chemicals, he grew cultures of the bacteria *Staphylococcus*.

One day in 1928, as he was working in his laboratory, Dr. Fleming noticed that one of the culture plates had mold growing on it. Many people might have thrown the plate away, thinking it was useless. But he noticed something startling. No bacteria were growing near the mold. Was the mold somehow killing the bacteria?

Alexander Fleming had just discovered penicillin.

d) How would you determine if the mold actually killed the bacteria?

Immediately, he started trying to separate the chemical that killed the bacteria from all the other chemicals in the mold. Unfortunately, he was unable to do so. However, in 1940, two chemists, Ernst Chain and Howard Florey, did manage to separate the chemical penicillin.

## Penicillin

Penicillin became a usable medicine with an outstanding ability to kill bacteria. It has saved the lives of millions. In 1945, Alexander Fleming, along with Ernst Chain and Howard Florey, received one of the highest awards in science— the Nobel Prize in Medicine and Physiology.

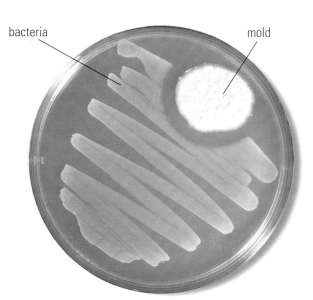

bacteria　　　　　mold

No bacteria will grow next to the penicillin mold.

## Case Study Questions

1. What did Alexander Fleming do to discover penicillin?

2. What award did Dr. Fleming win for his discovery? Do you think he deserved the award for what he did?

## Apply

3. Albert Szent-Gyorgyi wrote, "A discovery is an accident meeting a prepared mind." What do you think he meant? Was Dr. Fleming's discovery really accidental?

## Extensions

4. Is penicillin still as effective as it used to be? Research the present uses of the antibiotic.

5. Research a Canadian scientist such as Frederick Banting and Charles Best, the co-discoverers of insulin, or Emily Howard Stowe, the first woman to practise medicine officially in Canada, or Armand Bombardier, the inventor of the snowmobile. Non-Canadian scientists you may choose to study could include Marie Curie in physics, Jocelyn Bell in astronomy, or Jane Goodall in animal behaviour. Report to the class on the scientist you have chosen.

# Sherlock Holmes and the Scientific Method

THE AUTHOR OF SHERLOCK HOLMES, Sir Arthur Conan Doyle, was trained as a doctor. Not surprisingly, a considerable amount of science crept into his writings. In many ways, Sherlock Holmes used a scientific approach to solve mysteries. He systematically isolated variables and eliminated suspects until only one suspect and an explanation for the crime remained.

The large magnifying glass became his symbol for careful observation. No clue was too small.

Although challenging to read, the works of Conan Doyle provide an excellent example of how detectives use the scientific method.

---

**TRY THIS**

### Solving a Mystery

Read an approved mystery story and write a journal entry explaining how the sleuth used the scientific method to solve the crime. Use the Model for Scientific Investigations, presented on page 7, for reference. The following list of questions may help you with your journal entry.

Forming a hypothesis: How did the detective use:

• observation

• questioning

• predicting

Testing the hypothesis: How did the detective:

• control variables

• look for clues

• use scientific instruments

Evaluating the hypothesis: How did the detective:

• record observations

• identify trends or patterns

• interpret results

• draw conclusions

*Serratia marcescens*

# Science Sleuths

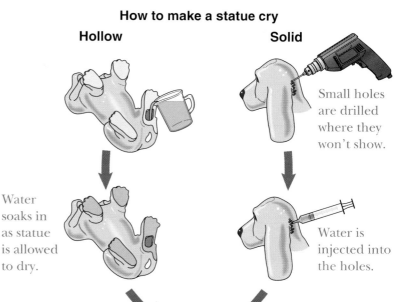

**How to make a statue cry**

**Hollow**

Water soaks in as statue is allowed to dry.

**Solid**

Small holes are drilled where they won't show.

Water is injected into the holes.

Small holes are scratched in the glaze.

Statue "cries" as stored water leaks out.

The similarity between sleuths and scientists is emphasized by many scientists. One scientific detective case took place in Italy in 1994. Claims that a porcelain statue could cry created tremendous public interest.

Luigi Garlaschelli, a chemist at the University of Pavia, has investigated many crying statues. He says hollow statues are the easiest to make cry. Because the statues are made from clay, they can hold a large amount of water. If the statue is exposed to air currents, the water quickly evaporates and the inside feels dry, but the clay still holds lots of water. A small scratch in the glaze on the outside provides an opening for this stored water to escape. If the tiny scratches are placed near the eyes, the statue appears to form tears.

Solid porcelain statues require more detective work. Garlaschelli has found tiny pinholes in the head of some statues, some of them cleverly disguised by folds of hair or crowns. If a small amount of water is injected into the hole, within a few minutes, tiny tears appear through the almost invisible scratch marks near the eyes.

Statues that weep red, blood-like fluids, are more difficult to explain.

There are ways to collect clues, however. If the fluid lacks hemoglobin, an oxygen-carrying protein, then it isn't mammalian blood. If it isn't blood, what is the red fluid?

A harmless bacterium that lives in warm, moist climates, *Serratia marcescens,* is known to grow on a variety of foods. Not only is this bacterium bright red, but so are the fluids it releases. Some scientists have pointed out that many incidents of blood appearing from statues occur during times of increased moisture in the air. They speculate that the bacterium may be responsible.

## SELF CHECK

1. In what ways do scientists act like detectives?
2. How do detectives use the scientific method to solve mysteries?
3. Give an example of a type of question that science is unable to answer.

## Journal Entry

4. Look back at your Getting Started activity about scientists. After exploring this unit, has your view of scientists changed? If so, in what way?

# Animal Research

ANIMAL RESEARCH USES animals to study surgery procedures, diseases, cures, and product safety, all of which usually relate to humans. Animals are used in both research and teaching.

The number of animals used each year is not known with any certainty, but estimates exceed 100 million, many of them mice and rats.

In health care, extensive animal experimentation is used to test drugs, cosmetics, and chemical and medical devices for usefulness, effectiveness, and toxic effects. Because non-human primates, such as chimpanzees, are similar to humans, they are valuable for studies on the eyes, blood, and the heart. The rhesus monkey is used for testing new surgical techniques.

Animal research has yielded valuable information. Experiments on chickens led to a better understanding of gout, a thyroid condition. Research using horses led to new treatments for respiratory diseases. Rats were used in the laboratory experiments that led to a cure for polio. Animals are currently being used in the study of AIDS, cancer, and glaucoma, an eye condition that can cause blindness.

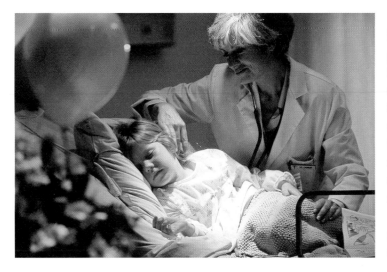

But animal experimentation has become increasingly controversial. Animal-rights groups say that animals have rights and that they should not be used in scientific experiments. Others feel there are alternatives to using animals, such as cell and tissue cultures or computer models. Still others feel that only certain animals, such as rats and mice, should be used for experiments, while other animals, such as monkeys, cats, and dogs, should not.

Animal research has saved the lives of many humans. But the price has been the lives of animals.

1. What are the benefits of using animals in research?

2. What are the problems with using animals in research?

3. What are the alternatives to using animals in research?

## Extension

4. Write a letter to the editor of a local newspaper that either supports or opposes the use of animals in research.

5. Research another ethical issue in science, such as genetic engineering or the use of growth hormones in animals. Present your research to the class.

## Journal Entry

6. During the preparation for the debate, did emotion affect your decision in any way? Explain your answer.

## TRY THIS

### Debate

Proposal: The use of animal experiments should be completely banned in Canada.

## Point

- Animals have rights. They don't benefit from the research, and they should not be forced to be part of the experiments.

- All life is important, not just human life. Just because we are humans doesn't give us the right to kill other animals so that we can live.

- There are alternatives to animal research.

- Many of the animals used in research are used for testing cosmetics and unnecessary drugs. Surely animals shouldn't die so that we have a new shampoo or a new colour of lipstick.

## Counterpoint

- The use of animals in research has led to a cure for many diseases.

- We kill animals for food; what difference does it make if we also use them for medical purposes?

- The alternatives to animal experiments are often not as good. For example, if you don't know everything about the body, any computer models you make will be faulty.

- Rats and mice are bred specifically for scientific research. Their use does not upset the balance of nature.

## What Do You Think?

- Are you in favor of the use of animals in scientific research? Would you favor animal research in some instances, for example, in medical research, but not in others, such as in cosmetic research? Why or why not? Research the topic thoroughly and prepare for a class discussion.

## Key Outcomes

Now that you have completed this unit, can you do the following? If not, review the sections in brackets.

Describe how scientists work. (1, 2, 16, 17)

Form and test scientific hypotheses. (2, 9, 10)

Provide an example of a scientific theory and explain why scientific theories are constructed and why they can change. (2, 9, 10)

Describe a scientific model for problem-solving. (2, 12)

Identify and form scientific questions. (3, 9, 13)

Use observation and all senses to collect data. (4, 5, 6)

Explain the limitations of observation. (4, 9)

Identify career opportunities in science. (7)

Identify chemical safety symbols and recognize potentially unsafe procedures in the laboratory. (8)

Explain the functions of a control and independent and dependent variables in an experiment. (10, 11)

Experiment by testing a hypothesis, making observations, and carefully controlling variables. (11, 13)

Communicate scientific information by way of data tables, graphs, and diagrams. (11, 13)

Use scientific models during an investigation. (11, 12, 13, 14, 15)

Design and conduct simple experiments to test a hypothesis. (13, 14)

Use technological thinking to create a device capable of moving objects. (15)

Describe a scientist's contribution to science. (16)

Discuss an ethical issue in science, describing strengths and limitations of scientific investigation. (18)

## Review Questions

1. For each of the following, write T if the statement is true. If the statement is false, rewrite it to make it true.

   **a)** All variables except one are controlled in an experiment.

   **b)** Scientific experiments can answer all the questions that we have.

   **c)** Scientific discoveries always happen through the use of the scientific method.

2. What are scientific theories? Why do they change?

3. Outline the steps you might take to investigate a scientific question.

4. List four ways that you could record and present scientific data. Beside each one, give an example of when you might use this method.

5. Provide an example of how a stereotype of a scientist could be misleading.

6. Construct a scientific question from each of the observations below. Present each question as a hypothesis.

   **a)** After I sit in the bathtub for a long time, my fingers get all wrinkled.

   **b)** After a candle burns, the mass of the candle decreases.

   **c)** I accidentally stuck my glove in the lake and after a few minutes my hand really felt cold.

   **d)** Salmon can find their home stream.

7. Explain why safety goggles should be worn in the laboratory if you are working with chemicals.

8. What type of safety precautions must be taken when you wipe up a spilled chemical?

9. Explain each of the following terms:

   **a)** Independent variable

   **b)** Dependent variable

   **c)** Control

10. Explain why a prediction is considered to be scientific only if it is testable.

11. Why are scientific models used?

## Problem Solving

12. The following graph provides evidence that the number of bacteria increases under a bandage. Examine the data and read the conclusion carefully.

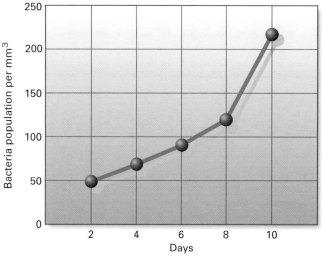

**Changes in bacteria population in a bandage**

Conclusion: The moisture in the bandage is responsible for the increased growth of bacteria.

   **a)** What other variables could account for the rapid increase in the number of bacteria?

   **b)** How would you go about eliminating the other variables?

   **c)** What advice would you give someone who is wearing a bandage?

13. Construct a scientific hypothesis for each of the statements below. Design a procedure that would allow you to test the hypothesis.

   **a)** Hot-air balloons fly farther on cold days than on hot days.

   **b)** A baseball will curve more when the cowhide covering is cut.

   **c)** Brand X toothpaste helps prevent tooth decay.

   **d)** Bread mold grows faster in your locker than on the table.

   **e)** Some brands of popcorn seem to have fewer "dud" kernels.

14. A student conducted an experiment to decide whether wood or rubber would give the best bounce in a gymnasium floor. The student dropped a basketball and a baseball from different heights. The basketball was dropped on wood and the baseball was dropped on rubber. Was this a controlled experiment? If not, how would you make it a controlled experiment?

15. The device below was designed to investigate which area of a baseball bat is best for hitting the ball. The baseball bat is attached to a gate hinge. The bat is raised, then released, causing it to strike a ball sitting on a tee. The bat hits the ball in a different place, depending on the height of the tee.

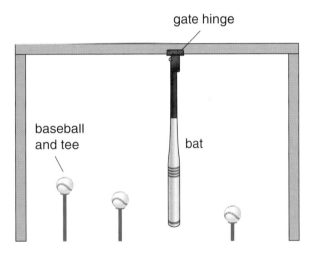

gate hinge

baseball and tee

bat

a) What is the independent variable?

b) What is the dependent variable?

c) List other variables that must be controlled during this experiment.

d) Make a prediction about the results of the experiment.

e) How would you change the procedure to improve the experimental design? Give reasons for each change that you suggest.

## Projects For Investigation

16. Interview a scientist about his or her work. Compare the image of the scientist often shown on movies and television to the person you met.

17. The following science puzzles will get you thinking about technological solutions.

a) Your task is to remove the metal thumb tacks from a glass of water without touching the water or pouring water from the glass.

Materials: Glass, thumb tacks, water, and magnet.

**b)** Your task is to lift the jar and the ball from the top of the table without touching the ball. The ball must not touch the table top once you lift the jar.

Materials: ball, jar.

**18.** Prepare a report on the use of science by magicians.

## Investigation Questions

**For 4: Science at the Scene of an Accident, page 10.**

1. What illegal activities did you see?

2. What day was it? Approximately what time of day was it? How do you know?

3. Who's to blame for the traffic accident?

4. How many bank robbers were there? What did they look like?

5. What was the name of the café?

6. What were the licence plate numbers of the cars involved in the accident? What colour were the cars?

7. Which of the following suspects was involved in the bank robbery?

8. Which of the following people was involved in the traffic accident?

### Extension

9. Compare the lists that group members made. Are the lists the same? Are there any observations that everyone made? Are there any observations by group members that contradict those of other members?

# Glossary

## C

**control:**

in an experiment, a method of ensuring that unknown variables are not affecting the results (p. 24)

## D

**dependent variable:**

in an experiment, a variable that changes as a result of changes in an independent variable (p. 23)

## H

**hypothesis:**

an explanation for observations that can be tested using an experiment (p. 22)

## I

**independent variable:**

in an experiment, a variable that is deliberately changed by the experimenter (p. 23)

## M

**model:**

an object, diagram, or idea that helps understanding; a small-scale test used to prepare for larger, more expensive future experiments (p. 36)

## S

**scientific question:**

a question that can be answered using scientific problem-solving; a scientific question may suggest a hypothesis, which can be tested (p. 8)

## T

**theory:**

a hypothesis, or set of hypotheses, that has been tested and is supported by experimental evidence (p. 6)

## V

**variable:**

in an experiment, anything that might cause a change in the outcome (p. 23)